THE ULTIMATE GUIDE TO STARTING AN EVENT USHERING AGENCY

UTIBE SAMUEL MBOM

Copyright ©2021

All rights reserved. No part of this publication may be reproduced, stored or transmitted, in any manner whatsoever without a written permission from the publisher. The only exception is of a reviewer who may quote short excerpts in their review.

ISBN: 9798746456229

Dedication

To the budding entrepreneur in the event ushering industry. This is for you.

Acknowledgements

First I would like to thank God almighty for everything. His mercy and love kept me till this very day.

I must thank my dear friend Mr Ukpong who stood by me through trying times.

I must also thank my pastor Akan Weeks, for his word and prayers.

I would also like to thank my team, Mirabeeque Ovations for doing their best and remaining world first class ushers.

My husband, Mr Samuel Mbom, deserve endless thanks for his patience and support.

My brother Michael should be given a cup load of coffee for being a good PRO.

And I must not forget to pay tribute to my mentor Inyene Kreative Consult of blessed memory.

Foreword

Nowadays, the challenge of organizing, strategizing, and ensuring the smooth running of an event drives many people to thrust the coordination of their events to professionals. And this makes event ushering service a worthwhile and lucrative business. There are a lot of people who would love to start a career in event ushering, but do not exactly know how to go about it.

The steps outlined in this book are carefully researched and written from many years of professional experience in the event ushering industry. And I personally believe that it will be helpful to the neophyte in the field, and the already established agency owners.

Contents

Title Page 0
Copyright ii
Dedication iii
Acknowledgements iv
Foreword v
STEP 1 viii
Evaluate the Competition viii
STEP 2 ix
Understand the Market ix
STEP 3 xi
Choose a Business Name xi
STEP 4 xiii
Outline your Company's Constitution xiii
STEP 5 xiv
Save up some Money xiv
STEP 6 xvi
Register your Business xvi
STEP 7 xvii
Create Membership forms xvii
STEP 8 xviii
Get an Office xviii
STEP 9 xix
Select Your Ushers xix
STEP 10 xxi
Special Training xxi

STEP 11	xxiv
Refine Your Style	xxiv
STEP 12	xxvi
Maintain Discipline	xxvi
STEP 13	xxviii
Appoint a Head Usher or Representative	xxviii
Clientele	xxx
Cost and potential earnings	xxxii
Media & Marketing	xxxiii
Rebranding	xxxvi
The Boss	xxxviii
Monetization of Content	xxxix
Excerpts from My Interview Session	xl
Photographs from Events	xliv
	xlix
ABOUT THE AUTHOR	liii

STEP 1

Evaluate the Competition

Before starting an event ushering agency in your town, you need to check the level of competition. How tough is the competition in the market you are venturing into? If the competition is too tough, you have two options. The first is to consider starting the business in an entirely different town, area, or location.

The second option is to take a critical look at other competitors, and find out what they lack, and then take advantage of any loophole found. For instance, if your local competitor uses female ushers for events, you may consider adding some male staff to your team. If they have workers who are dark and fair in complexion, you may try and make your agency exclusive to fair-skinned persons. If they charge exorbitant prices for their services, you may render your services at a fair and lowest possible price. If you cannot apply both options, then it is best to venture into another completely different business.

STEP 2

Understand the Market

After you have completed the previous step, the next thing to do is to speak with an already established individual in the industry. Local competitors will be disinclined to give away ideas. However, an entrepreneur who owns an event ushering agency in a town, location or area that is different from yours would be more willing to share startup advice with you, given that it would be impossible for you to compete with, outshine or steal their ideas. In my experience, the best thing to do is to relax and study the business. By doing so, you will acquire a firsthand experience and knowledge of the business.

Attend events, conferences, and seminars. Find out what an event ushering manager charge for every event. Go online and comb for everything related to ushering, events, clients and the minimum and maximum salary ushers get for every event. Also, learning the basics in the business is continuous because the business is more of management and coordination.

Any form of formal education and/or training in management, marketing, communication and planning will help a great deal. There are also schools and colleges in the country and abroad where the business can be learnt.

STEP 3

Choose a Business Name

A brand name is to a brand what a book title is to a book. A business name is the easiest thing to come up with. You can create a business name from your name or nickname. The name must be unique to you, meaningful, short and appealing, and in my experience, I think you need to be somewhat creative in order to come up with a catchy and sensational name. Whatever you choose to call your business, know that it must be free from vulgarity and obscurity. The length of the name should not exceed three words. For instance, I chose to call my event company, Mirabeeque Ovations. The meaning of Utibe is Miracle, so, the name Mirabeeque is derived from Miracle. When you add up everything, it means "a round of applause for Mirabeeque," and in another sense it means "give Mirabeeque your support." You can look up business-name ideas. The best platform to start is Pinterest.

The next thing to do after picking a business name is figuring out what your motto will be. Your motto should be able to state, in one sentence, what clients will benefit from opting for your services.

For instance, mine goes like this: "Mirabeeque Ovations: We make your event exquisitely memorable!"

Do not rush to pick a name and motto. Relax, and do a lot of brainstorming, research and experimenting, and see what works for you.

STEP 4

Outline your Company's Constitution

This is one of the most important steps you need to take in the journey of your career. This is done when you have finally decided to start a career in event ushering.

Write down your preamble, aims and objectives, mission and vision statements. State the rules and regulations of your group, and during group meetings, let your new members of staff go through them.

State clearly in the constitution the duties of an usher, the do's and don'ts, and other relevant instructions. After drafting them down, you need to print out as many copies as you can. Own a personal copy and keep the rest in a safe place for prospective members. If you do not know how to write a constitution, you can look up samples online.

STEP 5

Save up some Money

You need not be a billionaire in order to start an event ushering agency. What you need to do is to plan ahead of time. In some cases, your charismatic personality might be the only thing that is required of you. However, if you had some money somewhere, now is time to put it into good use. If you want to make your agency legitimate and unique, you must get it registered with the corporate affairs commission (CAC), for Nigerians. The registration fee is considerably high, so if your funds are not enough, you may seek support from well-to-do individuals in your town who are interested in innovative ideas, or you may as well remain unregistered, and still do the business.

If you do not have a car, or a bus, you will need to save up for transportation, because some clients do not include that in the quote. Also, you need to budget some money for sewing. The sewing of uniform is not mandatory, but necessary, in case an urgent job comes up. Sometimes clients will tell you what to wear and may as well cover the expenses, and sometimes they do not.

Furthermore, I would advise every beginner to be willing to spend money, because quality things, no matter how costly, are always the best choice.

STEP 6

Register your Business

Make your event ushering agency eligible by registering your business name. Secure a domain (your business name) for your website/blog, and consider opening a special business bank account. If you want your business transactions to be done online, sign up on PayPal or Payoneer, and add your debit card and bank account details. Creating a bank account for your business is great because it convinces your potential clients and customers that you are just not an average company owner, but a person who is worth doing business with.

Another way to project this image is by printing complimentary cards. A complimentary card consists of your name, the company's name, mail, logo and contact. Instead of using the antiquated method of writing down phone numbers and email, or doing a lame thing as dictating it for your clients to write, you simply slip your complimentary card into their hands and just walk away. Because of a minor thing as that, potential clients would regard you as a top-notch professional who knows and means business.

STEP 7

Create Membership forms

Create membership forms for those interested in being a part of your team. You can create one with Google forms, or you may ask a professional to assist you. After selling the forms to potential staff members, schedule a date for an interview. Set up a panel of experienced judges, especially those who know the business inside out.

Don't just pick random people for the job; let them pass through the process of buying forms and getting interviewed. Doing so will make them take the job seriously. Set the price for the forms. It should not be too expensive, and should cost between 8-10 dollars

STEP 8

Get an Office

As an entrepreneur, you need a permanent office in order to run this business smoothly and comfortably. If you have enough funds, rent a small room or convert your own room into an office. An office will serve as a meeting point between you and your clients.

Also, if there is an upcoming event, all you need to do is simply invite your ushers over to your office for a meeting. Perchance, if you become famous in future, your office might just be the right place for journalists to stroll in for an interview.

STEP 9

Select Your Ushers

You can build your event ushering agency by starting with fifteen to twenty members of staff. Be very choosy when it comes to recruiting ushers. View your potential workers from the perspective of a hardcore psychologist. Screen them thoroughly and give your final verdict. Don't ever employ anyone out of sentiment and pity; it ruins business. Give everybody what they deserve.

You may utilize the following criteria to choose your ushers:

- Height
- Body shape
- Legs
- Gait
- Voice
- Age
- Experience
- Educational level, background, and qualifications
- Character and body language

Don't choose beauty over brains, even though you are not recruiting university professors; it is important that they should speak good, simple, and correct English. They should be beautiful and handsome. They should have a great smile. They should be approachable and cordial. They should be passionate about their job. And above all, they should have the ability to think and act fast.

STEP 10

Special Training

The next step after interviewing and selecting the ushers will be to organize a special training session for them. Some of the basic things they should be taught are:

- ❖ Good communication skills

This covers verbal and written communication and listening. It is about being concise, clear, and focused; being able to tailor your message for the audience and listening to the views of others.

- ❖ Ability to work under pressure

This is about keeping calm in a crisis and not becoming too overwhelmed or stressed.

- ❖ Confidence

In the work place you need to strike the balance of being confident in yourself but not arrogant, but also have confidence in your colleagues and the company you work for.

- ❖ Organisation

This is about showing that you can priotize, work efficiently and productively, and manage your time well. It is also good to be able to show employers how you decide what is important to focus on and get done, and how you go about meeting deadlines.

- ❖ Good interpersonal skills, including the ability to collaborate with management, team members, clients and customers.

You will need to prove that you are a team player but also have the ability to manage and delegate to others and take on responsibility. It is about building positive working relationships that help everyone to achieve goals and business objectives.

- ❖ Commercial awareness or business acumen

This is about knowing how a business or industry works and what makes a company tick. Showing that you have an understanding of what the organization wants to achieve through its products and services, and how it competes in the marketplace.

- ❖ Problem solving

You may need to display an ability to take a logical and analytical approach to solving problems and resolving issues. It is also good to show that you can approach problems from different angles.

❖ Enterprise and entrepreneurial skills

Spotting gaps in the market, suggesting ways to improve processes, or coming up with new ideas are all signs of an entrepreneurial approach. You don't have to set up your own business to make use of your enterprise skills.

STEP 11

Refine Your Style

A famous writer once said that style is the answer to everything. Indeed, he was right, because every business person/owner has his/her own style or way of doing their business, and that is where the difference lies. And, if you are looking to start your own ushering agency, you have to be stylish, choosy, creative, and exceedingly unique. Style sets you apart from others. It is your eternal trademark. With style, you are the bona fide owner of your art. No one else creates like you, and you create like no one else.

Clients are after that diminutive quality in your art that sets you apart from other entrepreneurs — this is where style and genius comes in. Style could mean the general appearance of your ushers, the makeup your ushers wear, their hairdo, their shoes, the costume and its design, the colour of the uniform, especially if it blends with or does not blend with the colour of the event.

As an event ushering connoisseur, it is incumbent on you to pay rapt attention to every detail. Your style must be unique to you alone. The body language of your ushers also falls into the category of style. Do they smile or frown at guests? Can they stand for two or more hours? Is their oral English good? How do they greet and treat the guests? If these and other things are ticked right, then you will get a lot of acclaim, endorsements and referrals.

STEP 12

Maintain Discipline

There are so many misconceptions about event ushering and event ushers. One of them is that people think ushering business is sex work in disguise, and the most alarming of all is when some clients and guests try to pay agency owners for a one night stand with female ushers. Those kinds of clients and guests seriously need mental help, and any decent event coordinator would never agree to that. There is a big difference between event ushering and sex work, and agency owners should make this clear.

A good name, they say, is better than silver and gold. The people who last in this business are those with good and impeccable reputation. You should know better than risking the business you spent years to build. Remember that decent clients with good morals will never hire a disreputable team. The message here is that it is better to stay clean with fewer clients than getting involved in things that will besmirch your good image.

As an agency owner, it is your duty to caution and advise your ushers on the kind of dealings or relationship they have with the clients and guests. They should be told that offering services outside the business is highly prohibited and against the rules and regulations of the group. Furthermore, make sure to drop anyone who fails to adhere to this rule, and keep those who abide by them.

STEP 13

Appoint a Head Usher or Representative

Note that the head usher is an extension of you. He/she plays your role when you are either absent or incapacitated. The head usher knows virtually everything about the organization, and how to run the business. He/she is like a consigliere in the Mafia. And because of this, you must appoint someone you can trust; someone who will never reveal your business strategies to your local competitors.

The head usher must be outspoken, honest, disciplined and humble. He/she must respect other ushers in the group irrespective of his position and privilege as one who plays the major role. However, the members of staff must treat the head usher with respect. Even when the CEO is engaged elsewhere, his/her orders must not be flaunted or taken for granted.

When the CEO is away, the head usher will be the one to organize group meetings, inform other ushers about upcoming events, get the uniforms or take them to the tailor's.

When you are not in the office, he/she must cover for you, interact and schedule meetings with clients, advertise your business, and supervise other ushers. Finally, it is incumbent on the head usher to give account of everything that happened during an event, and be responsible for each and every one of them.

Clientele

Clients believe what you show them, not what you tell them. The duty of a client is to pay for services rendered. And the duty of a service provider is to render top-notch services.

One important thing you must know is that a business moves when it moves the client. Think about your clients first before thinking about your business. When you take their problem as your problem, you've got no problem. In fact, when you serve your clients right, you are saving your business. You must understand that clients are the reason why you are still in the business, so why should their needs be toyed with? They should be satisfied with your services. There are some who would annoy and stress you out, but you must either endure or ignore. As a starter in the field of event ushering, you must understand that patience is key. If you do not have it, you might quit the job earlier than you had bargain for.

Your success as an agency owner partly depends on your relationship with clients. For you to work successfully with clients, you need to take note of each and every of their temperaments or dispositions. There are some who are melancholic or choleric, while others may be sanguine. You also have to let your representative (head usher) understand this fact.

When a client demands for a quote, he/she is asking for a budget breakdown, i.e. the amount of money he/she intends to pay for your services. You must state a fair price, and the reason for this is that the majorities of other ushering agencies are lining up for, or may be looking for an opportunity like yours, so be careful not to pass any job up. Be cordial to your clients, for when you do so, they will not only refer other clients to you, but will keep you in their inner circle of trust.

Cost and potential earnings

The kind of event you are coordinating, the choice of your client on the outfit of your ushers, the location of the event, and the professionalism of your ushers, among other factors, will determine your cost and charges. Having considered the required factors, you can charge a minimum of between 5,000 and 10,000 Nigerian naira per usher, which is equivalent to 13.11-26.23 United States Dollar for an hour conference/seminar.

However, for other functions, such as wedding ceremonies, birthday parties, child dedications, the salary may reduce, unlike two, three, and five-day conferences which costs between 10,000 and 25,000 Nigerian naira per usher. This is one of the reasons why you should not afford to miss big events, because the pay is always good and high. Finally, after getting paid, you may deduct 10-20% from your usher's salary as your commission.

Media & Marketing

There are two kinds of marketing; offline and online marketing. Focus on both, and your business will spring to its feet. Marketing is the lifeblood of every legitimate business.

Event ushering business requires lots and lots of marketing and exposure. And if you want your brand to stand out, you have to do everything possible to be in the spotlight.

Get to work or pay an expert to design you a quality flyer. And then print as many copies as you can. When you have an event, instruct your ushers to keep at least three flyers on every table in the hall. Assign some of your ushers to go out for publicity. Send them to public and private establishments, such as hotels, event centers, fast foods, offices, etc.

Get interviewed on the radio or TV about your event ushering agency, or pay someone to do a Jingle for you. Advertise your brand on popular newspapers and magazines.

Anytime you go for an event, ask your client if it is proper to place your roll-up banner at the entrance of the hall. Make the banner attractive with large and readable fonts, including some recent photographs.

Make customized T-shirts with the name and logo of your brand on the front or back, and let your ushers wear this during informal events, such as birthdays and get-togethers. Make quality name tags for your ushers for easy identification by the guests.

Before an event starts, gather your ushers together for group photographs. Use your mobile phone camera (of the highest resolution) or hire a professional photographer to take good and detailed shots. If there are guys in your team, let them stand on each end. Remember to make videos too.

Urge your ushers to promote your brand by hyping the agency, and make sure they don't overdo it. They should say things like, "We are the best brand." And they should also quote the motto (insert yours), "We make your event exquisitely memorable!" Make live videos while the event is ongoing.

Capture important moments, i.e. while the ushers are serving dignitaries and guests at an event.

The next thing you need to do is to go online. List your services on social media pages, such as Twitter and Instagram. You may use the format below:

Our services:

- ✓ Corporate Ushers
- ✓ Commercial models
- ✓ Tour guides
- ✓ Event planning
- ✓ Bridesmaids
- ✓ Logistics

   And more

Setup a Facebook page, Instagram page, Twitter page, LinkedIn page, etc. Create a YouTube account for your brand and start uploading all the pictures and videos you took during events. Add relevant hashtags and keywords to your uploaded content and tag your ushers and other event ushering agencies. You can look up the best hashtags for event ushering on Google. Create sponsored posts (ads) on Facebook, Twitter, and YouTube to reach millions of potential clients. Create a website or blog and upload all of your contents. Get your ushering agency visible on Google by signing up for a Google My Business account. Google My Business promotes and lists your business online so that potential clients can find you easily.

Make it mandatory for your ushers to post pictures of the event they went for on their Facebook timeline, Twitter and Instagram pages.

Look for popular brands and sponsor. When you do that, your brand name may soon become a household name as it will be mentioned and listed among other famous brands.

But in all these, you have to know that no matter how boomy your online campaign is, however, at the end of the day, you cannot really buy fame with advertising, but by successfully coordinating a number of successful events, and building good relationships in the industry. When you go by this simple rule, your reputation will soon tower over that of your competitors.

Rebranding

Rebranding, when done properly, can bring a dead brand back to life. It is often said that change is the only thing that is constant, and when it happens in the world of business, everything becomes anew. After three to four years in office as an event ushering agency owner, you may discover that some of your members of staff are no longer in your team anymore. You may discover that some uniforms are beginning to wear and tear from excessive use. You may find out that some ushers are not as passionate about their job as they were before. You may also wonder why clients are not in need of your services anymore. It is about time you do something. You need to start over again, but this time, you are getting started as a pro. The hour where you need to repackage everything has come.

Sewing new uniforms will be the first step. Look for an expert tailor and let him/her handle this business. The second thing you need to do is to employ new members of staff. You may still retain some old members, because they are to teach the recruits basic things about ushering. Change the looks and faces on your roll-up banner, flyers, etc., to the current ones. Schedule a date for a photo shoot. Update your social media pages with pictures from the photo shoot and make sure that anything updates you make on the social is directed to the public. Announce to the public once again that you have rebranded your team, and ask for patronage. Do not let your passion fade into oblivion; get your brand into the spotlight.

The Boss

A lot of people do not seem to know that I have given a new meaning to the word, 'Boss'. They think it means ordering people around. To me, that cannot be true, because a leader's purpose is to lead, and not to command.

To begin a career in event ushering agency, you must allow the business to pass through you, and you too, should allow yourself to pass through the business. You have to be genuinely interested in the industry. Event ushering business is not for the procrastinator, neither is it meant for the soft and weak. It is for those willing to take risks, bear the pain and pressure, and work around the clock. It is for those who can make clients change their minds about certain decisions.

As a leader, you have to be a good talker, charismatic, fit and persuasive. You have to be cautious when dealing with clients, and able to remain calm under pressure. As a leader, you have to keep to time. If an event is scheduled for 8AM, make sure that your ushers arrive at the venue earlier than the stipulated time. Don't be at loggerheads all the time with your ushers. Once in a while, be jovial with your ushers. If an usher gets ill on the job, allow them to take some rest. When they look stressed out, don't frown, give them a reassuring smile that they will soon be relieved. Compliment them for their little effort.

Monetization of Content

Do not just own an event ushering agency for nothing. If you have a great personality, and a huge online following, then you are more than eligible to make some extra money. Monetize your content; during events, such as wedding ceremony, anniversaries birthday party, etc., make live videos on YouTube, Facebook and other social media platforms. You can earn up to 100 dollars per 10,000 views. You can also use the Amazon affiliate program to promote other brands and earn money. You can place ads on your website with the Google AdSense program. Use your Payoneer or Paypal account as the funding source for your income.

Earning extra cash as an entrepreneur is important because these extra bucks could save you from mismanaging your hard earned salary. The extra cash you earn from monetization could pay for your event ushering costume, transportation fare, refreshment during meetings, and other arising needs. Seeking professional advice on monetization is just the best thing for you to do in order to get started and earn that good money.

Excerpts from My Interview Session

Interviewer: I have heard wonderful things about you. A few days ago, I stumbled upon a picture of you and a group of young girls in uniform. Can you let us in on what you do?

Utibe: The girls in the picture are my ushers. I own an event ushering agency or you may call it "Company." Clients hire us for their event, and, at the end of the day's job, we get paid for our services.

Interviewer: In what capacity, like…what kind of services do your ushers offer?

Utibe: Well…their job is to stand at the door and welcome the guests, show them to their seats, help them locate the ticket stand, help them find the restroom, distribute event programme to guests, and run some errands for the client, if any.

Interviewer: What about refreshment. Do they take care of that too?

Utibe: I know a lot of agency owners who are against that, but I do not see anything wrong with my ushers serving food. If there are not enough Caterers, they can offer a helping hand. Though, it is not part of the job, but I'm okay with that.

Interviewer: Impressive! How often do you get an ushering gig?

Utibe: Three times a week. It can last through the week if it's a five-day job.

Interviewer: What is the pay like?

Utibe: It depends on the kind of event. I charge a huge sum for seminars and conferences, especially when it has to do with state or political functions.

Interviewer: How long have you been in this business?

Utibe: Approximately seven years.

Interviewer: Do you have clients from another state?

Utibe: Yeah! A lot of them. Particularly in Lagos, Calabar, and Abuja.

Interviewer: Who pays for transportation and accommodation?

Utibe: Some clients do, but most of the time it's from my purse.

Interviewer: Tell us how this career of yours started. Your brand name, Mirabeeque Ovations is gradually becoming a household name. You are the most finest in the industry, and you are widely known for your professionalism, give us some inspiration.

Utibe: In my early twenties, I worked as a model and usher for Inyene Kreative Consult, a big agency as at that time. The experiences I had shaped and prepared me for the future. Though, I wasn't interested in starting up an event ushering agency. It was a friend who talked me into it. He said to me, "You have worked for several agencies for the past four years, wouldn't it be nice to start yours and become your own boss?" Indeed, I was motivated by his pep talk, but I doubted myself. As an introverted person, I thought I would not be able to interact with clients and all of that. Where will I even get the money to start up this business? I thought to myself, but you know, I remembered the words of one writer named Paulo Coelho, "When you want something, all the universe conspires in helping you to achieve it."

Interviewer. That's some encouraging words, ma'am. You are an indeed an inspiration.

Utibe: Thank you.

Interviewer: Now, apart from your ushering agency business, what else do you do? Do you have plans or passion for other things?

Utibe: Well, I'm a graduate. I majored in Psychology. My dream is to pursue my masters abroad. I am passionate about helping the poor and needy. That is why I started a foundation, dedicated to helping less privileged children. You know, children are a priority in the society.

Interviewer: That is a great ambition ma'am, and I commend you for that.

Utibe: Thank you.

Interviewer: What is your foundation called?

Utibe: Mirabeeque Foundation

Interviewer: Another Mirabeeque? That name seems to pop up everywhere. Why is it so special to you?

Utibe: Actually, the meaning of my name is Miracle, so it's a coinage. I know it sounds French, but that is how I want it to be.

Interviewer: As a professional, what do you think is the future of event ushering?

Utibe: I believe that event ushering is a coming thing, and it's extremely profitable. It will grow and expand in the future. There are several event ushering agencies in Nigeria, and the number keeps going up. One thing I foresee in this industry is that if enough service providers accumulate bad reports and reputation, the government might decide to put a ban on it.

Interviewer: Do you have a word for budding agency owners?

Utibe: I would advise the up-and-coming agency owners to stick to their passion. They should never be scared or overwhelmed by the number of their local competitors. If they are not winning today, there is always another day to get up and try again. After all, Rome wasn't built in a day, but they worked on it every single day.

Photographs from Events

ABOUT THE AUTHOR

Utibe Samuel Mbom has over 7 years' experience in event management industry. She has a good grasp of clients' need, fears and desire and is well accustomed to the Nigerian and international event outlook and has commensurate success at it. She also has an extensive network of professionals providing similar services and products in the industry. She is a certified business consultant and project management professional.

www.ingramcontent.com/pod-product-compliance
Lightning Source LLC
Chambersburg PA
CBHW050314220526
45465CB00005B/1981